Stillwater Trout Fishing

Tony Whieldon

Introduction by Russ Symons

WARD LOCK LIMITED · LONDON

First published in Great Britain in 1988
by Ward Lock Limited, 8 Clifford Street
London W1X 1RB, an Egmont Company.

Printed and bound in Italy by New Interlitho, Milan

British Library Cataloguing in Publication Data

Whieldon, Tony
    Stillwater trout fishing. – (Fishing
    skills).
    1. Still waters. Trout. Angling
    I. Title II. Series
    799.1'755

    ISBN 0-7063-6639-5

Contents

Introduction

Stillwater trout fishing can, by and large, be divided into two types. Firstly, there is the abundance of naturally-occurring lakes containing brown trout, of which the Irish and Scottish lochs are by far the most highly regarded and famous. Secondly, there are the reservoirs and purpose-made lake fisheries. These rely on the artificial stocking of rainbow trout to keep up the quantity of fish necessary to attract the modern angler who, in return for his or her money, expects at least a sporting chance of catching trout.

The fisheries stocked with rainbow trout have come a long way since Blagdon was the first reservoir to be stocked with rainbows in 1904. No better choice of reservoir could have been made, and it soon became evident that not only did the rainbows flourish, but they co-habited harmoniously with the naturally-occurring brown trout. From that date onwards, the foundations were laid for the stillwater trout fishing that we cherish and enjoy today.

Tony Whieldon illustrates all the information needed by the angler taking up fishing for trout on the fly, whatever type of stillwater he is fishing on. However, as any experienced angler will tell you, a lot can also be learnt by actually getting out on the water to fish, and observing other anglers.

Some will be the clever ones; others will have that natural knack to be at one with nature; then there are those who think they are clever. Finally, there is the majority: fishermen who use their native intelligence, and work hard to improve their fishing skills, loving every minute of it, and revelling in every day that they guess right or recognize some small point that has escaped the attention of other fishermen.

It would be easy for me to describe at length the traditional joys of presenting a diminutive dry fly on a floating line; and that heart-pounding moment as a trout sips the delicate concoction of fur and feather, so lovingly tied during the dark winter evenings when the wind and rain lashed against the window-panes. It is right that this aspect of fishing should be mentioned, because no one can truly be called a flyfisherman unless he ties at least some of his own flies.

Perhaps this is where stillwater trout fishing begins to demand special skills, because although the traditional dry and wet fly skills of the river fisherman overlap and transfer to stillwaters, the stillwater trout angler has evolved fly patterns and skills peculiar to stillwaters, and in particular to the rainbow trout.

Some of these flies and methods do not sit easily with the traditional fly-fishing purist. Nevertheless, like it or not, they are part and parcel of today's flyfishing scene. Some of these flies are more akin to spinning lures than flies, and the heavy rods and lines necessary to cast them would not be out of place in pursuit of fish many times the average weight of trout. However, that said, there is a perceptible trend today back towards the lighter rod and line.

Tony Whieldon is an angler who far prefers the joys of deceiving a trout with the cunning of expert fly-tying and presentation over the repetitive long cast and fast retrieve of the habitual lure fisherman. However, part of the skill involved in catching fish is to recognize and respond to the almost subliminal clues with which trout indicate their behavioural patterns, from month to month, day to day, even from hour to hour. And if the trout are responsive only to a flashy lure — then so be it!

Tony has succeeded in capturing within these pages a distillation of the fishing skills that are needed for different types of stillwaters, and which we all work so hard to acquire. His finely-tuned sense of observation, which makes him such a talented artist and, indeed, such a joy to fish with, and his understanding of fishing techniques, have combined to produce a book that is infinitely rich in information yet clear and comprehensible at the same time. He has pointed the way for those who want to learn, as I have learned from fishing with him.

Russell Symons,
Plymouth, Devon.

January, 1988

Stillwaters

WILD MOORLAND LAKES

RESERVOIRS

SMALL MAN-MADE FISHERIES

Weather — the effects of wind

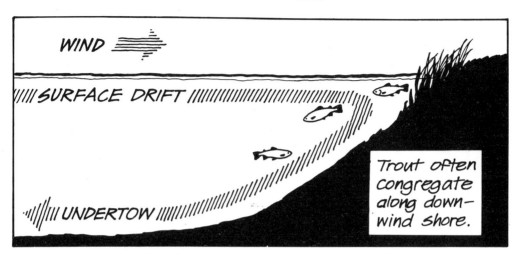

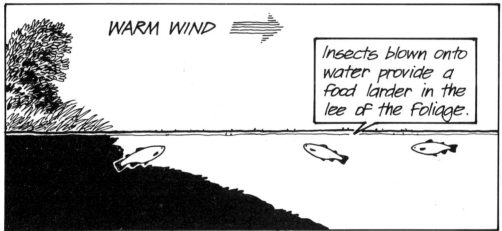

Rods, reels, lines and leaders

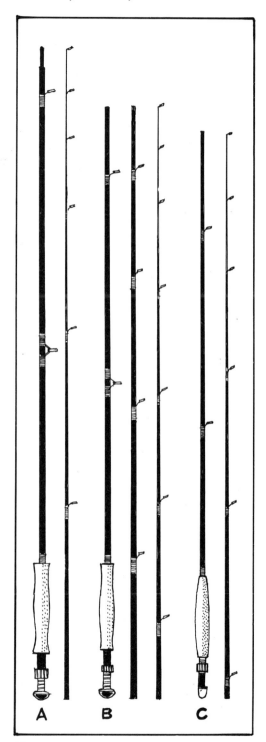

RODS

(A) 9ft 6in (2·90m) carbon rod with a line rating of 7–9 for bank fishing and lure fishing from a boat.

(B) 11ft (3·35m) carbon rod with a line rating of 5–7 for loch-style fishing from a drifting boat.

(C) 7ft (2·15m) carbon rod with a line rating of 4–5 for floating line work from bank or boat.

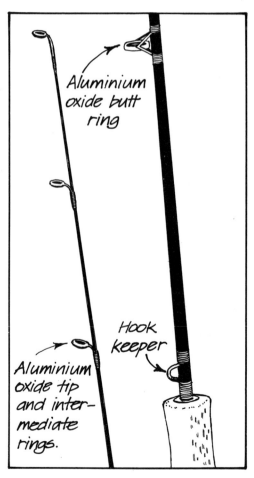

Aluminium oxide butt ring

Hook keeper

Aluminium oxide tip and intermediate rings.

A   B   C

REELS

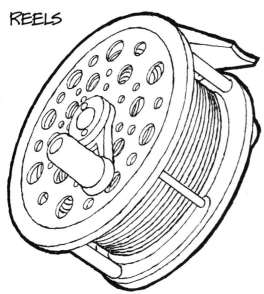

Wide drum multiplier reel with line and backing for use with the 9ft 6in (2·90m) rod.

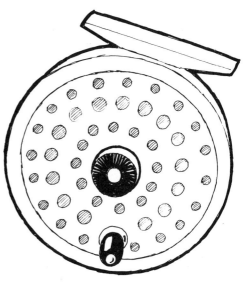

Lightweight magnesium, single action reel holding a 4-5 line, for use with the 7ft (2·15m) carbon rod.

Standard drum, single action reel holding 5-7 double taper floating line for use with the 11ft (3·35m) loch-style rod.

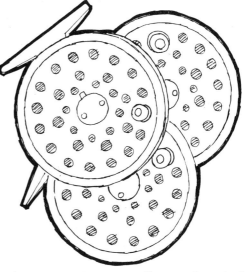

A selection of lines loaded on to spare spools or reels will be needed for the 9ft6in (2·90m) rod. eg., WF Floater, WF Sinker, or Shooting Head Floater and Sinker and DT Floater.

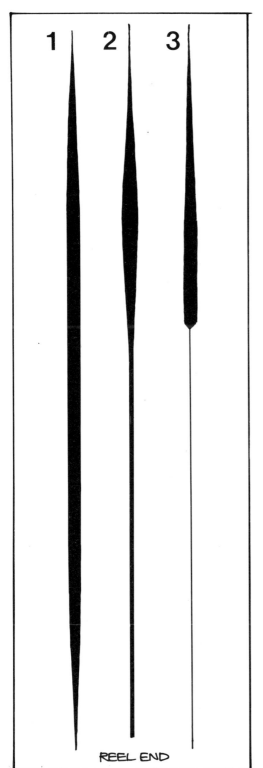

REEL END

1 DOUBLE TAPER (DT)
  The standard length for a full fly line is approximately 30yd(27.43m). The DT is ideal for delicate presentation when fishing at close to medium range, or when loch-style drift fishing from a boat.

2 WEIGHT FORWARD (WF)
  Longer casts can be made with this line, but it does have the drawback of creating a disturbance as it hits the water. However, it is a very useful line for general shore fishing.

3 SHOOTING HEAD
  This set-up is usually a home made affair comprising 35ft(10.50m) of DT fly line and at least 50yds(45.5m) of braided monofilament or solid monofilament shooting line, plus backing.
  Shooting heads are also available from some tackle shops.

The profiles shown previously can all be obtained in different densities – here they are.

1 FLOATING (F)
   For fishing a dry fly or a wet fly in the upper layers, or a weighted nymph in the lower layers. Some floating lines have a sinking tip (SF).

2 NEUTRAL DENSITY (N)
   Extremely slow sinking line with a multitude of uses when the upper layers and shallow water is being fished.

3 MEDIUM SINKING (S)
   For searching different depths and fishing a lure or a nymph at mid water.

4 FAST SINKING (S)
   For fishing close to the bottom in medium-depth water.

5 ULTRA FAST SINK (UFS)
   For fishing close to the bottom in deep water.

6 LEAD CORE
   For exceptionally deep work in deep lakes. Especially useful when trailing lures very close to the bottom, from a slow – moving boat.

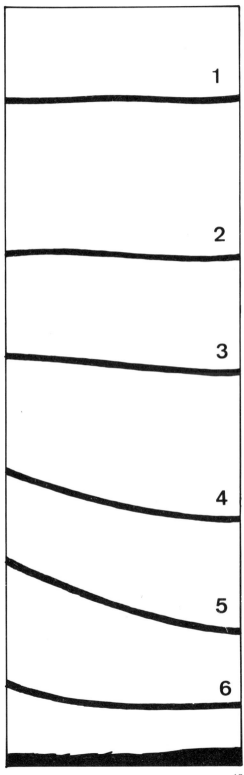

LOADING THE REEL

As the overall length of a fly line is no more than 30 yd (27 m), it is advisable to increase the volume of line on the reel by adding several yards of backing. The amount of backing needed will depend on the size of the reel. To find the answer, wind the fly line on to the spool; attach the backing to the line then wind the backing on to the reel until it lies about ¼ in (6 mm) beneath the housing supports. Remove the backing and line from the reel, reverse, and rewind, backing first. Attach the backing to the spool with the knot shown below.

LINE TO BACKING

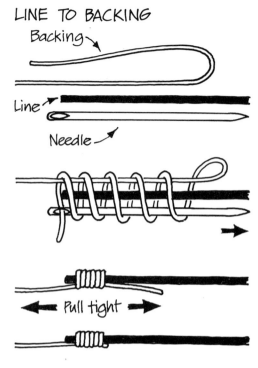

LINE TO LEADER

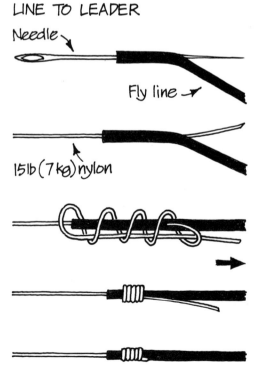

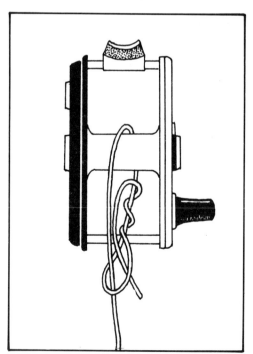

LEADERS (Butt end)

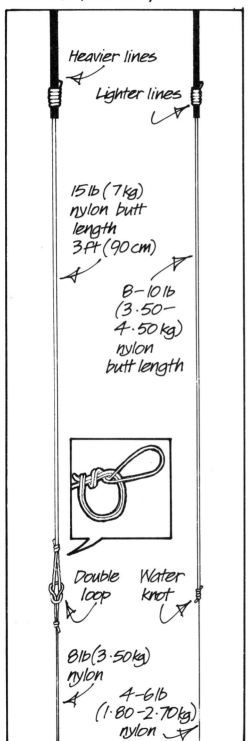

Heavier lines

Lighter lines

15 lb (7 kg) nylon butt length 3 ft (90 cm)

8–10 lb (3.50– 4.50 kg) nylon butt length

Double loop

Water knot

8 lb (3.50 kg) nylon

4–6 lb (1.80–2.70 kg) nylon

COMPLETE LEADERS

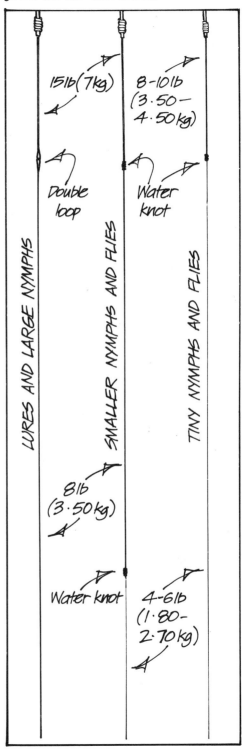

15 lb (7 kg)

8–10 lb (3.50– 4.50 kg)

Double loop

Water knot

LURES AND LARGE NYMPHS

SMALLER NYMPHS AND FLIES

TINY NYMPHS AND FLIES

8 lb (3.50 kg)

Water knot

4–6 lb (1.80– 2.70 kg)

Droppers can be added to the leader at any time, with a four-turn water knot.

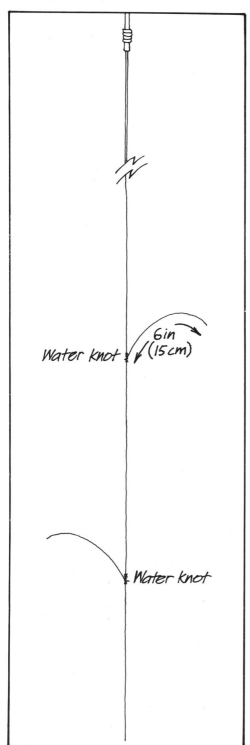

Water knot ↙ ↓ 6in (15cm)

Water knot

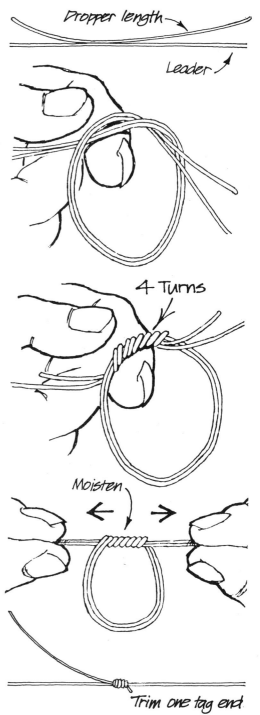

Dropper length

Leader

4 Turns

Moisten

Trim one tag end.

CONNECTING A SHOOTING HEAD

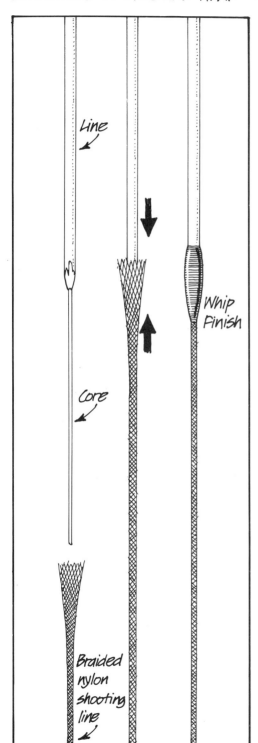

Line

Core

Whip Finish

Braided nylon shooting line

POWERGUM

The inclusion of this material in a leader permits very fine points to be used even when large trout are present.

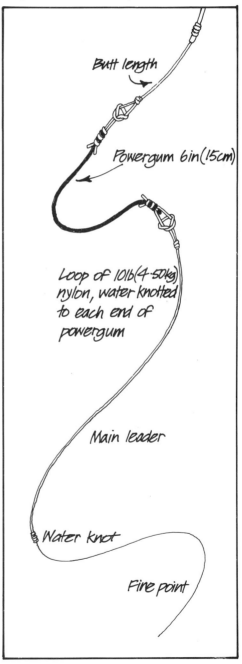

Butt length

Powergum 6in(15cm)

Loop of 10lb(4·50kg) nylon, water knotted to each end of powergum

Main leader

Water knot

Fine point

Casting a fly

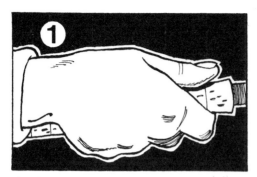

Hold the rod with the thumb on top of the handle.

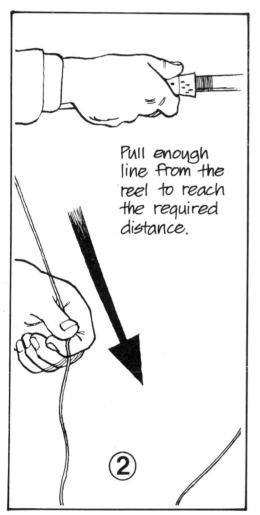

Pull enough line from the reel to reach the required distance.

Hold the line between the handle and the butt ring.

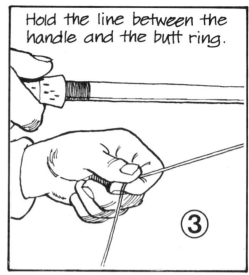

Lift the rod quickly but smoothly, and at the same time pull on the line.

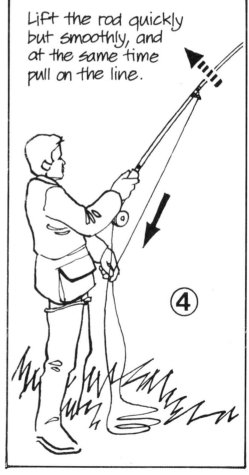

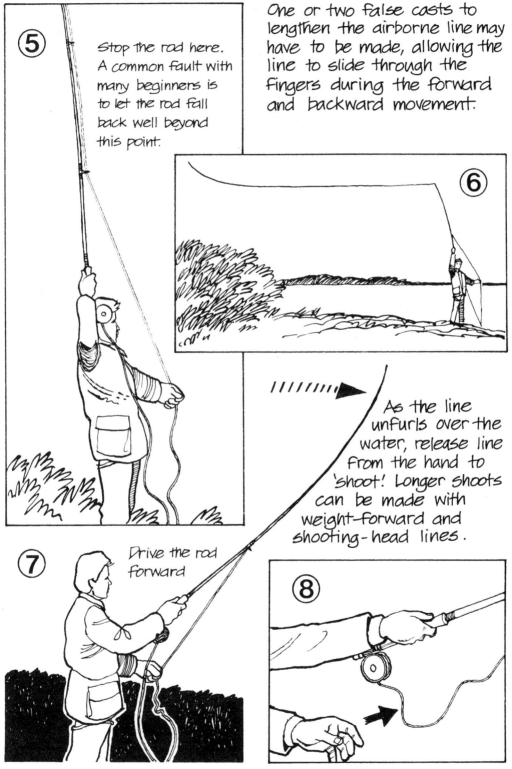

⑤ Stop the rod here. A common fault with many beginners is to let the rod fall back well beyond this point.

One or two false casts to lengthen the airborne line may have to be made, allowing the line to slide through the fingers during the forward and backward movement.

⑥

As the line unfurls over the water, release line from the hand to 'shoot'! Longer shoots can be made with weight-forward and shooting-head lines.

⑦ Drive the rod forward

⑧

Species of trout

BROWN TROUT

RAINBOW TROUT

BROOK TROUT

Brown trout (Salmo trutta fario) are indigenous to the British Isles and Europe.

Rainbow trout (Salmo gairdneri) were introduced to Britain and Europe in the 1880s and are used extensively to stock stillwater fisheries.

American brook trout (Salvelinus fontinalis) is a char, introduced from North America, which can be cross-bred with both brown and rainbow trout. A brook/brown trout cross is known as a 'tiger trout!'

The stillwater trout's diet

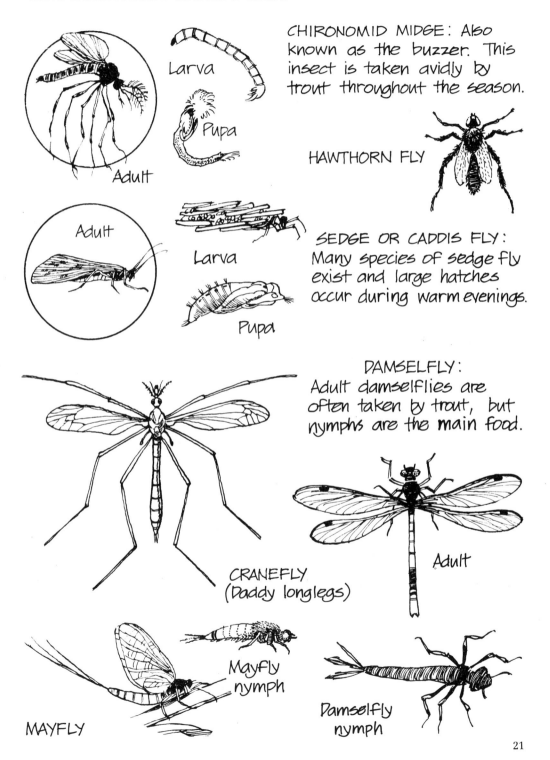

CHIRONOMID MIDGE: Also known as the buzzer. This insect is taken avidly by trout throughout the season.

Larva

Pupa

Adult

HAWTHORN FLY

Adult

Larva

Pupa

SEDGE OR CADDIS FLY: Many species of sedge fly exist and large hatches occur during warm evenings.

DAMSELFLY: Adult damselflies are often taken by trout, but nymphs are the **main** food.

CRANEFLY (Daddy longlegs)

Adult

Mayfly nymph

MAYFLY

Damselfly nymph

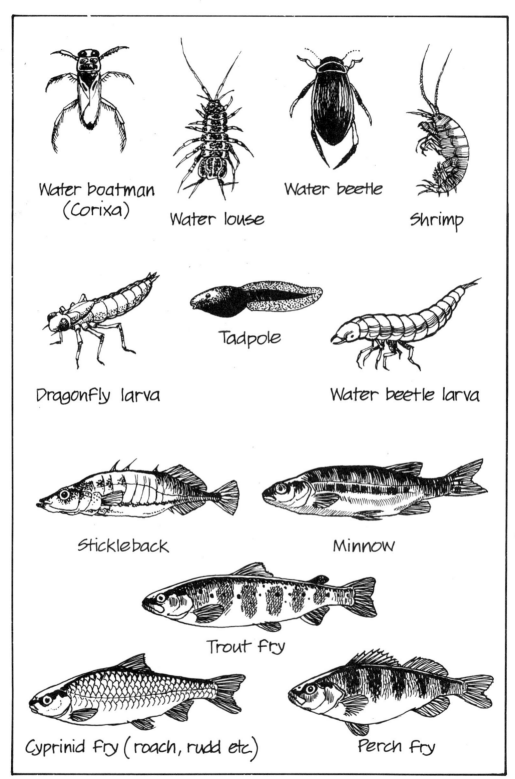

Water boatman
(Corixa)

Water louse

Water beetle

Shrimp

Dragonfly larva

Tadpole

Water beetle larva

Stickleback

Minnow

Trout fry

Cyprinid fry (roach, rudd etc.)

Perch fry

Changes through the year

Early season

As some small, stillwater fisheries remain open the whole year through (there is no close season for rainbow trout) the angler could well be casting his flies on New Year's Day; an early start indeed!

The best approach at this time of year is to fish the fly or flies in the deepest area of the lake, close to the bottom.

EARLY SEASON FLIES

VIVA

JACK FROST

MONTANA NYMPH

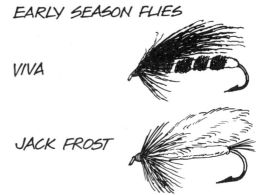

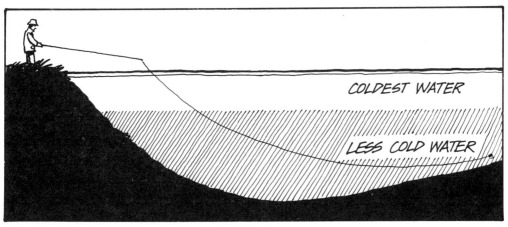

COLDEST WATER

LESS COLD WATER

Weed growth is minimal at this time of year and flies can be retrieved slowly, close to the lake bed.

However, a quick inspection of the hook is advisable after every cast as bits of detritus have a habit of becoming impaled on the point.

Although the tucked half-blood knot (a) is reliable, and widely used, it does allow the fly to hinge into a fixed position which could result in bad presentation. Alternatives are the turle knot (b) and the loop (c), both of which hold the fly rigid. Small wire clips (d) are available and ideal for larger imitations.

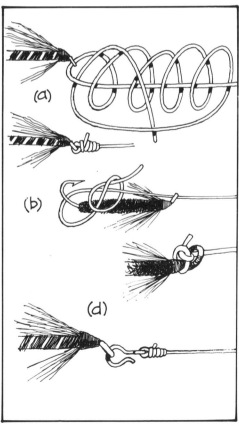

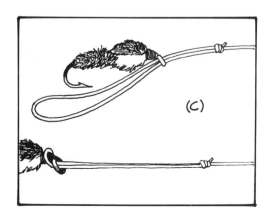

A pair of old leather gloves with the finger tips cut away provide protection for the hands during raw early-season conditions. A mere turn down of the wrist is all that is needed to keep the fly mobile.

Holding the rod tip at the correct level above the water surface will make visual take-detection easier.

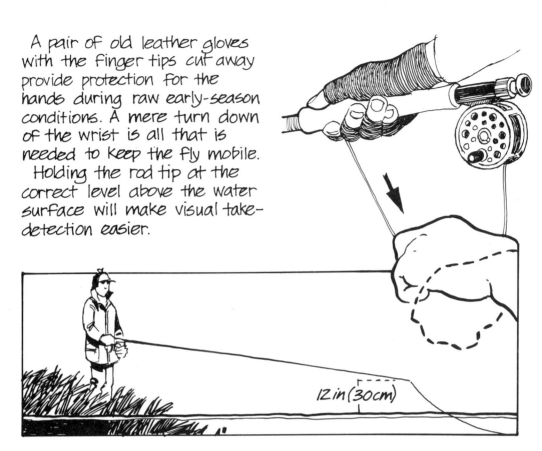

12 in (30cm)

Holding the rod at an angle to the line will lessen the risk of a snap-off if a trout makes a sudden hit-and-run attack.

Warmer weather tactics

April and May (unless the winter has been extremely hard) will produce some tangible evidence that underwater life is astir after its winter dormancy. A floating line can now be used with confidence as trout will be more widespread.

Fishing with a floating line and a long leader, furnished with one, two or even three imitative patterns of underwater bug is usually referred to as nymph fishing, and is a very satisfying way of taking trout. However I feel that the angler should not develop a narrow-minded or puritanical attitude to this style, and should be prepared to use any concoction of fur and feather, within reason, and call it a nymph. After all, even the most delicate creations made at the fly-tying vice cannot compare with nature's ultra-fragile and translucent underwater creatures.

IDEAL CONDITIONS FOR NYMPH FISHING

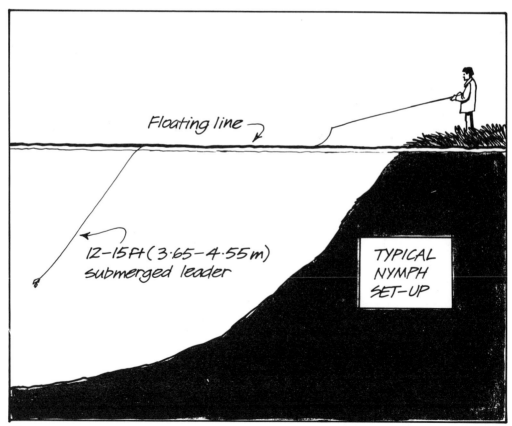

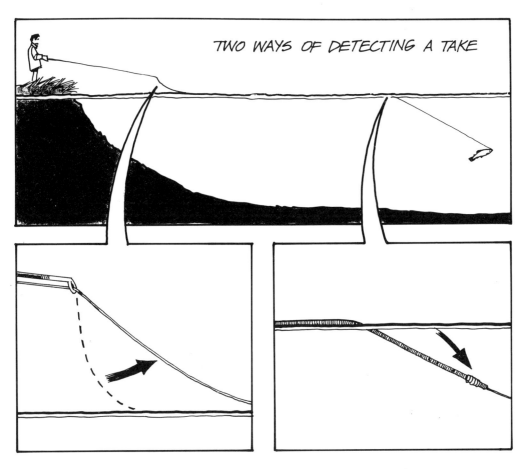

TWO WAYS OF DETECTING A TAKE

An excellent take indicator can be made from a length of a fluorescent plastic drinking straw.

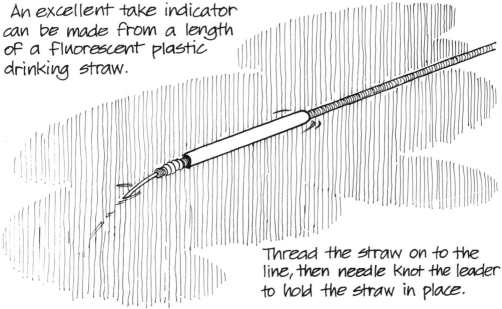

Thread the straw on to the line, then needle knot the leader to hold the straw in place.

RETRIEVING A NYMPH

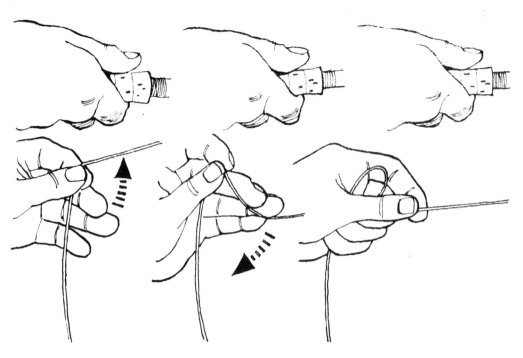

DRIFTING A NYMPH

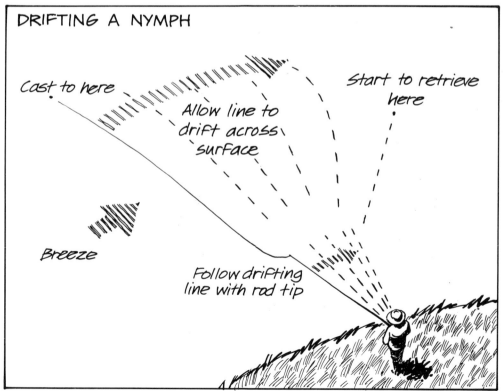

Cast to here

Allow line to drift across surface

Start to retrieve here

Breeze

Follow drifting line with rod tip

HOOK SIZES FOR DRIFTING A NYMPH

16-10

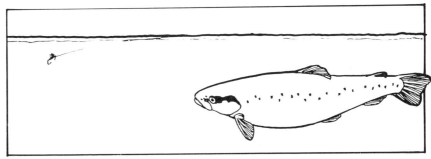

In or just beneath the surface film

10-8

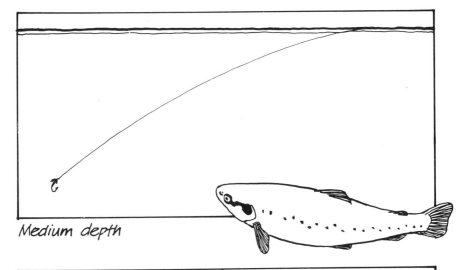

Medium depth

8-6
or smaller,
weighted
patterns

Deep

Retrieved or drifted nymphs can also be very effective using the dropper system.

Small nymph

Small nymph

Large or leaded nymph

If the water is clear and steeply-shelving near the bank, it pays to adopt a low profile during the last part of the retrieve.

A trout will often follow a fly almost into the bank, only to shear off at the last moment as it sees the angler standing against the skyline.

Nymphs and pupae

Sedge Pupa

Midge Pupae

Damselfly Nymph

Amber Nymph

Montana Stone

Persuader

Iven's Nymph

Corixa

Mayfly Nymph

PVC Nymph

Cove's
Pheasant Tail

Damsel Wiggle Nymph

Leaded Shrimp

Pheasant Tail Nymph

Chompers

Collyer's Nymph

33

The magic of May

May produces the trout's first glut of food in the shape of the hawthorn fly (Bibio marci). This is a terrestrial insect, and at times the hatch is so prolific that dense clouds of the large black insect fill the air. Stocked fish which have been reared on a diet of high-protein pellets sample this feast, but it is the wild fish of the upland lakes and reservoirs that respond most avidly, packing on weight in a frenzy of feeding for a week or so until the hatch peters out. If the wind is favourable the hawthorns are blown on to the water and quickly devoured by the cruising trout.

Natural hawthorn fly and imitations

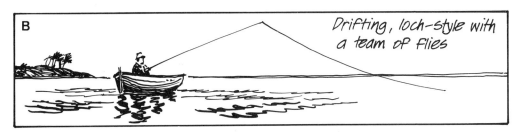

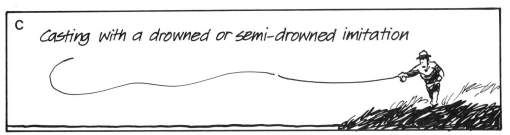

Back cast aimed high

Situation 'A' can present problems if the bank rises very steeply, so often the case on upland lakes. The best approach here is to use a long rod (the one recommended for loch-style boat fishing) and a double-taper 5-7 line. This outfit will reduce the number of hang-ups on gorse bushes, heather or bracken.

An alternative approach in this situation is to cast at an angle of about 45° to the shore. Trout will often be feeding fairly close in if the water is deep enough and many fish can be covered by working gradually along the bank.

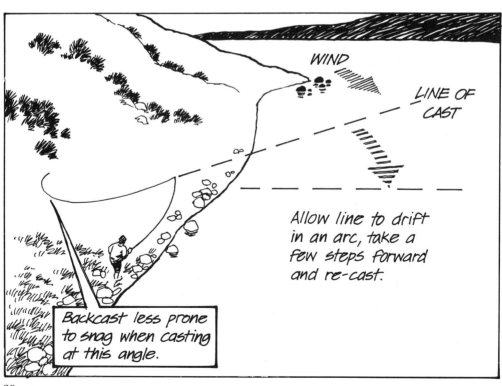

WIND

LINE OF CAST

Allow line to drift in an arc, take a few steps forward and re-cast.

Backcast less prone to snag when casting at this angle.

Dry flies

Black Gnat

Hawthorn

Hares Ear

Grey Duster

Knotted Midge

Alder

Coch-y-Bonddu

Baigent's Black

Walker's Sedge

G and H Sedge

Greenwell's Glory

Pheasant Tail

Daddy Longlegs

Coachman

Iron Blue Dun

Blue Upright

Dark Varient

Wickham's Fancy

Red Spinner

Silver Sedge

Loch-style

This popular, traditional method is performed by repeatedly casting a short line and a team of wet flies ahead of a drifting boat. May is an ideal month to start loch-style fishing, especially if the hawthorn fly is on the water.

① Using an 11 ft (3·35 m) rod, cast a double-taper floating line, with a rating of 4–7, two rod lengths ahead of the boat.
② When the flies are in the water, lift the rod through an arc from A to B, thus imparting a smooth, continual retrieve to the flies. Keeping in touch with the flies by pulling line with the free hand may also be necessary.
③ Flick the line back and repeat the process.

WIND ➡

①

DRIFT ➡

POSITION AT POINT B

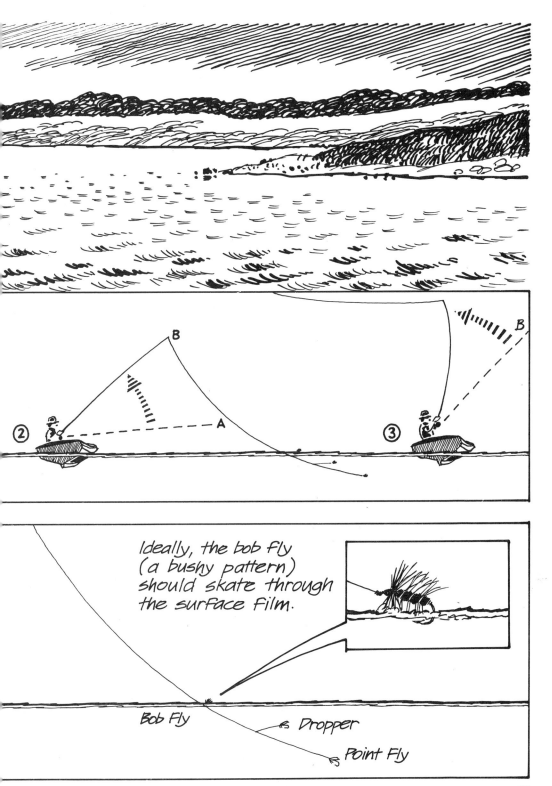

Ideally, the bob fly
(a bushy pattern)
should skate through
the surface film.

②   A   B   ③   B

Bob Fly   Dropper

Point Fly

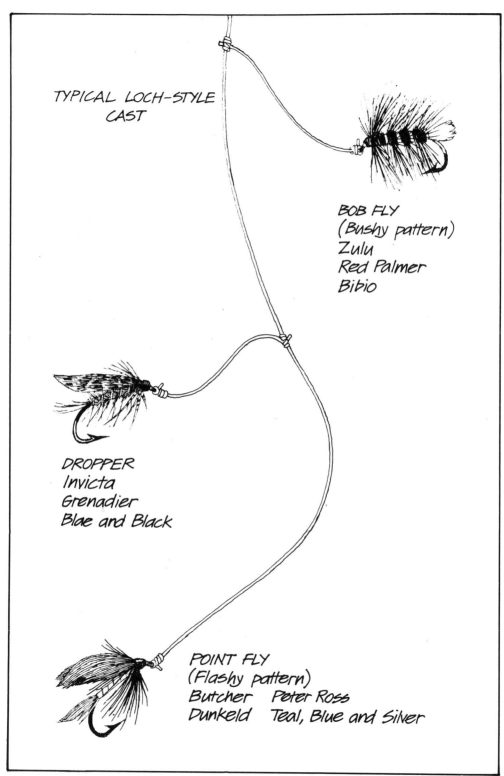

TYPICAL LOCH-STYLE
CAST

BOB FLY
(Bushy pattern)
Zulu
Red Palmer
Bibio

DROPPER
Invicta
Grenadier
Blae and Black

POINT FLY
(Flashy pattern)
Butcher   Peter Ross
Dunkeld   Teal, Blue and Silver

WIND

Drogue

In order to slow the passage of the boat and hold it broadside-on to the wind, a drogue will have to be used.

WIND

WHERE TO DRIFT
On upland lakes where the water is relatively acid, subsurface life is usually confined to the shallower areas bordering the shoreline.

Line of drift

WIND

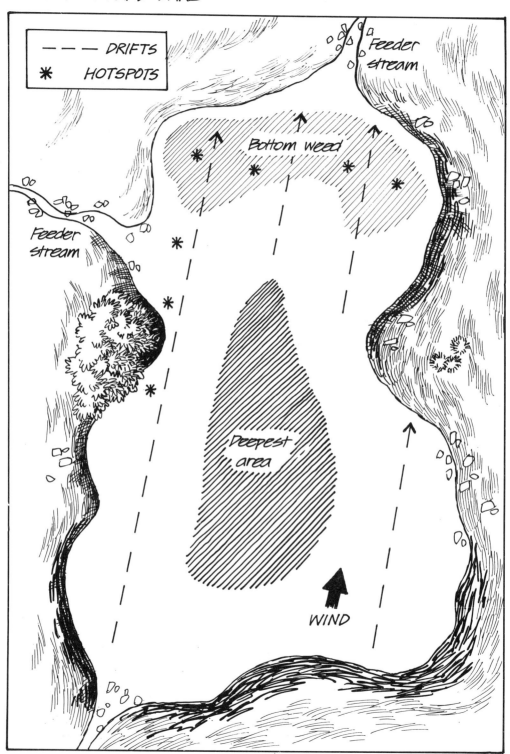

Lowland lakes with water having a more alkaline content will provide a larger choice of drifts as well as producing larger trout. However, the anomaly does present itself in some highland lochs, where the trout can average 2lb (0·90kg).

CHOICE OF LINE WEIGHT

With a gentle breeze, just enough to keep the boat moving, a No. 4 will provide perfect control.

Stronger blows will require heavier line such as No. 7.

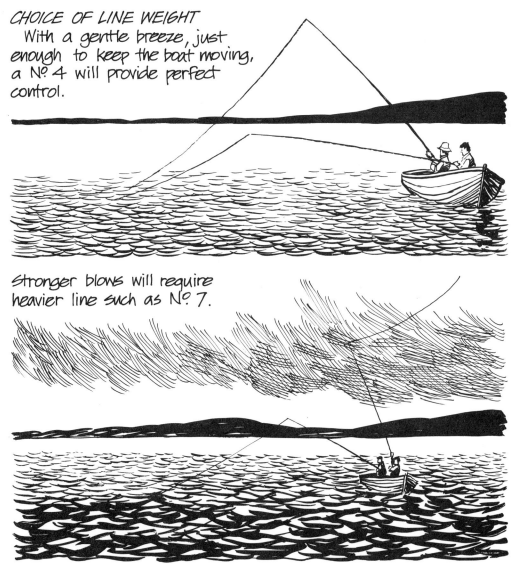

WIND

DRIFT

The wind may not always be favourable for a natural drift, but with the aid of an experienced companion the boat can be held, by sculling the oars, so that it drifts parallel to the shoreline.

When a fish has been hooked, bring it around to the windward side of the boat as soon as possible, where it can be played out and netted without the risk of the boat running over it.

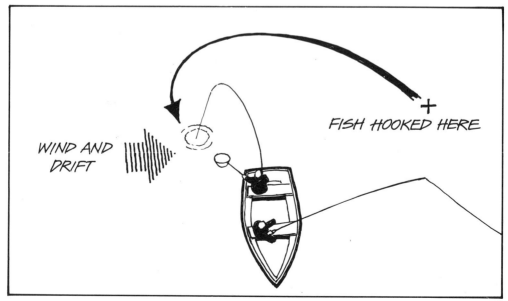

WIND AND DRIFT

FISH HOOKED HERE

Traditional wet flies

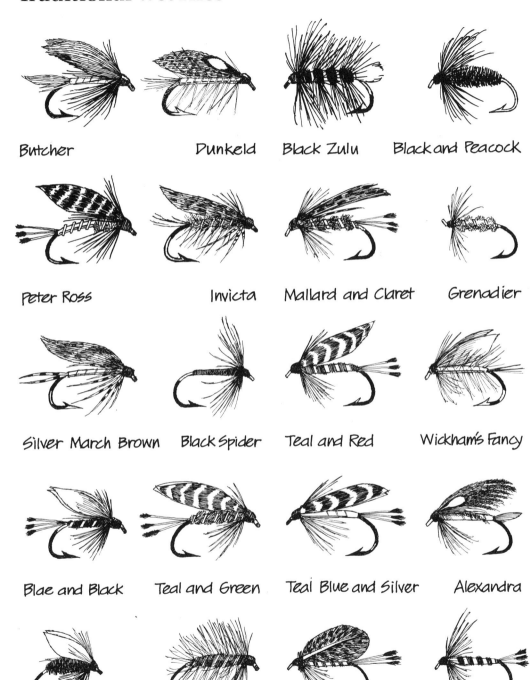

Butcher   Dunkeld   Black Zulu   Black and Peacock

Peter Ross   Invicta   Mallard and Claret   Grenadier

Silver March Brown   Black Spider   Teal and Red   Wickham's Fancy

Blae and Black   Teal and Green   Teal Blue and Silver   Alexandra

Coachman   Red Palmer   Parson Hughes   Black Pennell

Other boat fishing techniques

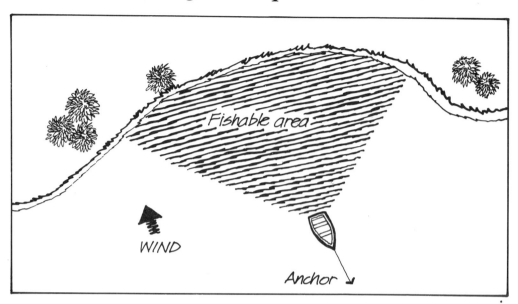

Small bays into which the wind is blowing are usually good fish-holding areas, especially if the lake bed supports any form of weed growth.

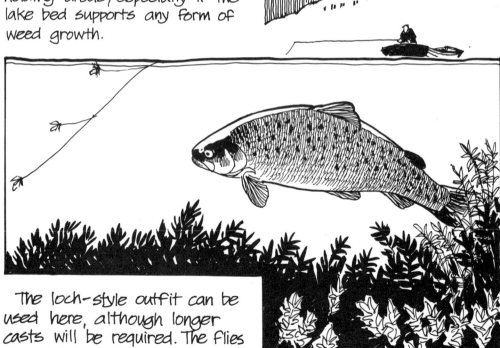

The loch-style outfit can be used here, although longer casts will be required. The flies should be retrieved nymph-style.

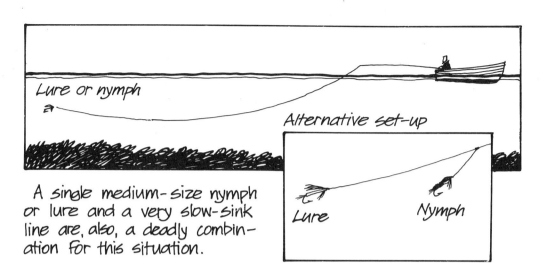

Lure or nymph

Alternative set-up

Lure

Nymph

A single medium-size nymph or lure and a very slow-sink line are, also, a deadly combination for this situation.

Lure fishing from a drifting boat

Although the traditional loch-style is the best method for catching fish which are near the surface, it is the deeply-presented lure that will score when trout are feeding closer to the lake bed.

PROCEDURE FOR FISHING A LURE FROM A DRIFTING BOAT

The boat is allowed to drift, with the aid of a rudder, bow first, downwind.

Each angler then casts, with a sinking line, at right angles to the boat.

WIND

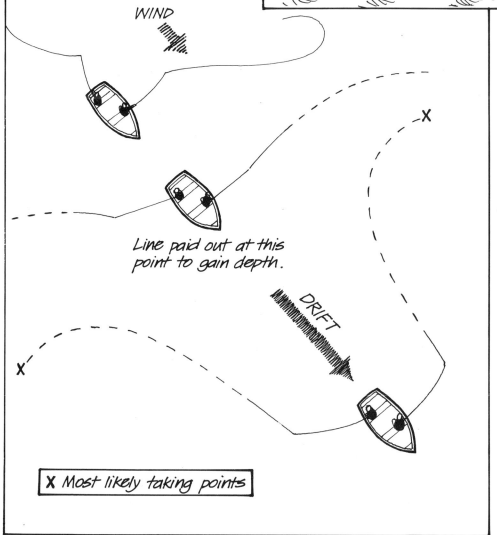

WIND

Line paid out at this point to gain depth.

DRIFT

X

X

X Most likely taking points

June, July and August

Early mornings, and evenings, provide the cream of the sport at this time of year, although excellent fishing can be had throughout the day if the sky is overcast.

Hatches of midge will be prolific, therefore it is logical to set up a rod in conjunction with a floating line and fish with an imitative pattern near the surface.

During periods of very hot, sunny weather it is wise to set up a standby rod which is equipped with a sinking line. This outfit can then be used if the fish retire to deeper water during the middle of the day.

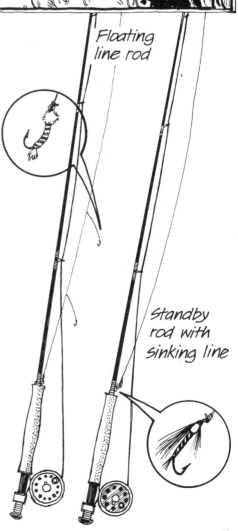

Floating line rod

Standby rod with sinking line

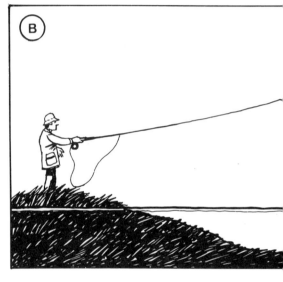

(A) On large reservoirs where the lake bed slopes gradually over large areas of shallows, long casts will be needed to cover midge-feeding trout. A floating weight-forward or shooting head line and a 9ft 6in (2·90m) carbon rod will be required here.

(B) Where trout are feeding closer to the shore the use of a double-taper line will be possible, allowing the angler to present the flies in a delicate manner.

(C) In certain situations, usually on small fisheries, trout will be feeding on midge pupae very close to the bank. A 7ft (2·15m) carbon rod and 4-5 double-taper line is the perfect combination for this exciting form of fishing.

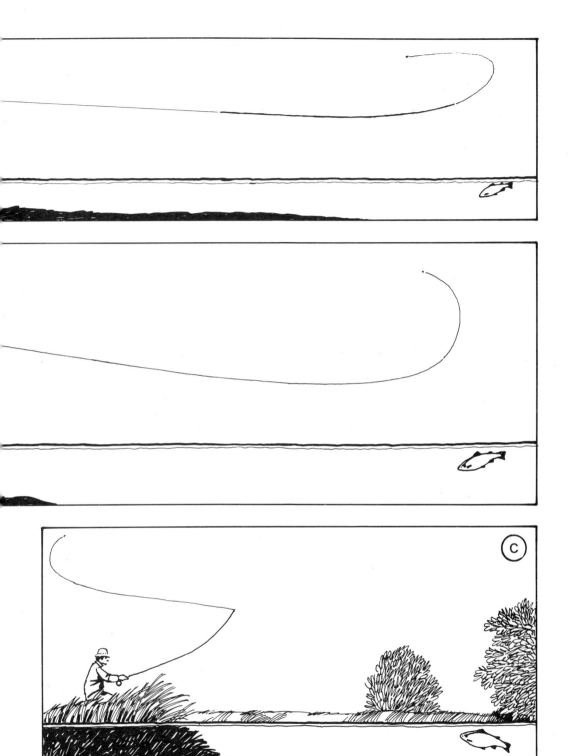

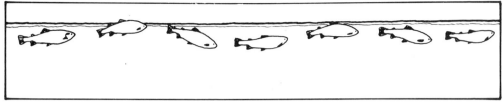

TYPICAL SWIMMING PATTERN OF A TROUT FEEDING ON MIDGE PUPAE

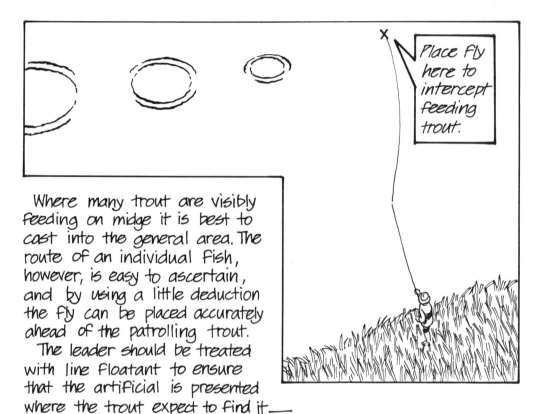

X

Place fly here to intercept feeding trout.

Where many trout are visibly feeding on midge it is best to cast into the general area. The route of an individual fish, however, is easy to ascertain, and by using a little deduction the fly can be placed accurately ahead of the patrolling trout.

The leader should be treated with line floatant to ensure that the artificial is presented where the trout expect to find it—

—in, or just under the surface film.

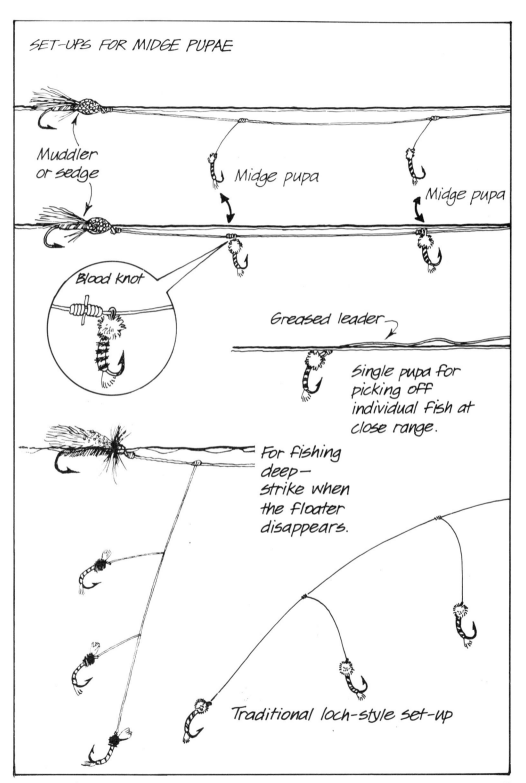

SET-UPS FOR MIDGE PUPAE

Muddler or sedge

Midge pupa

Midge pupa

Blood knot

Greased leader

Single pupa for picking off individual fish at close range.

For fishing deep— strike when the floater disappears.

Traditional loch-style set-up

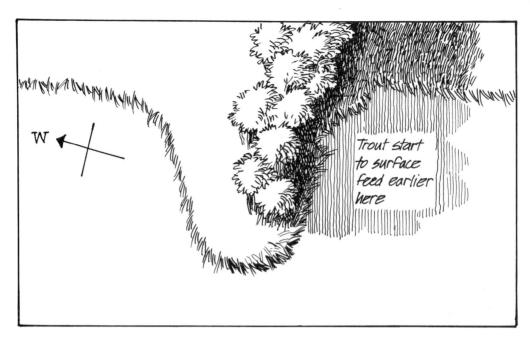

Trout start
to surface
feed earlier
here

W

Bright, calm sunny days during June, July and August do not provide ideal conditions for surface fishing. On such days, fishing deeply with a nymph or lure will be the only resort. However, midge and other insects continue to hatch, covering the surface with pupa, emerging adult insects and dead and dying terrestrial gnats and beetles.

Trout surface-feeding usually starts with the setting of the sun, but in areas of shadow on the east side of trees, it may start an hour earlier. Situations like this often provide the opportunity to indulge in some really close-in fishing with a light rod and line.

Bright, sunny days with a gentle, warm south-west or west wind provide a larder of insects in the surface film at the downwind end of a lake.

With the setting of the sun and the dying of the wind, trout will start to show in this area and will be easy to see against the backdrop of the sun's afterglow. A long rod and light line are the best combination for this situation, as it will often be an advantage, in the fading light, to lift the line off the water and cast quickly to a particular trout with the minimum of false casting.

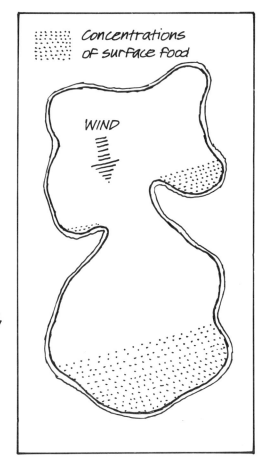

Concentrations of surface food

WIND

There will be times when evening-rising trout seem to ignore tiny offerings such as artificial midge pupae. This can be extremely frustrating. However, it is probably due to the fact that the trout do not see the artificial. A lure such as a Sweeny Todd or a Viva, fished with a floating line and retrieved just beneath the surface, usually has the desired effect.

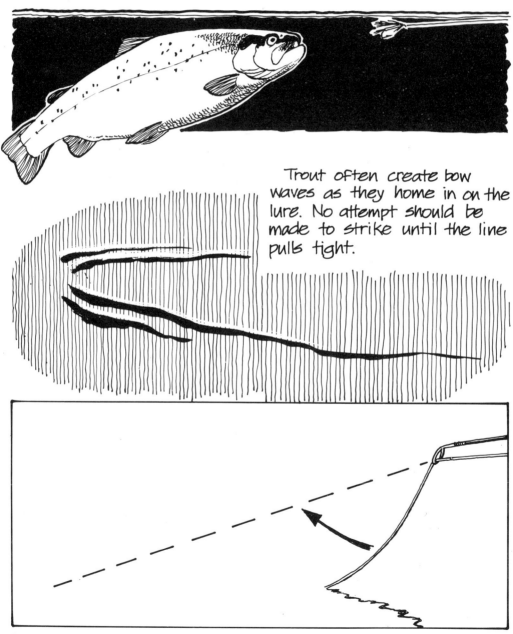

Trout often create bow waves as they home in on the lure. No attempt should be made to strike until the line pulls tight.

Warm summer evenings also provide the opportunity to fish a floating sedge imitation.

Sedge patterns can be fished static or drawn along the surface to assimilate the scuttling action of the natural insect.

Yet another effective fly to employ at dusk, or even after dark, if fishing is permitted, is a large white imitation ghost-swift moth.

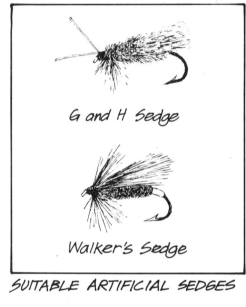

G and H Sedge

Walker's Sedge

SUITABLE ARTIFICIAL SEDGES

Fishing a sedge pupa

This pattern is a general representation of the many different sedge pupae found in most still-waters. During the summer months, the natural swims to the surface, or to the shore, in order to undergo the final transformation and become an adult sedge fly.

The artificial can be fished at mid-water, or near the bottom with a sinking line ....

.... or just under the surface with a floating, sink-tip, or very slow-sinking line.

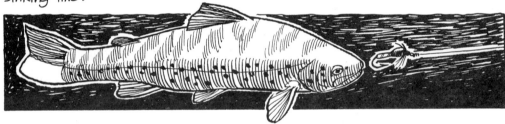

Retrieve the pupa at a medium pace, with long steady pulls, and a pause here and there.

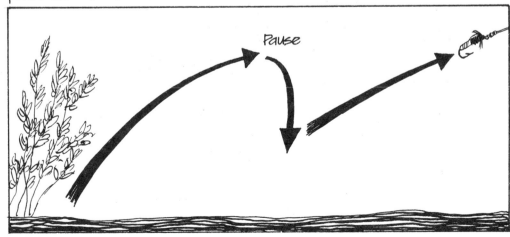

Pause

Fishing a damselfly nymph

During the early part of the season this pattern can be fished, very slowly, along the bottom. Shallower bays, where weed is prolific during the summer, are the most likely areas to attract the natural nymphs, as they feed largely on decaying vegetable matter.

During the warmer months the nymphs are far more active and wriggle to the surface, whereupon they proceed to swim towards the shore or surface weed in order to hatch into adult damselflies. To simulate this activity, fish the artificial just under the surface with a fairly fast retrieve, on a floating line.

Where there are rushes or reeds, it is often more productive to cast and retrieve along the shoreline.

Fishing a corixa

This pattern imitates the lesser water-boatman which spends most of its life near the bed of the lake, but has to rise to the surface in order to replenish its air supply.

Two patterns have developed to represent this little bug. The leaded version, which can be fished via a floating or a sinking line close to the bottom...

... and the buoyant (plastazote) version, which has to be fished with a sinking line.

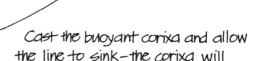

Cast the buoyant corixa and allow the line to sink—the corixa will float on or near the surface.

When the line is retrieved, the corixa will dive towards the bottom, imitating, in a very life-like manner, the action of a water-boatman as it swims back to base.

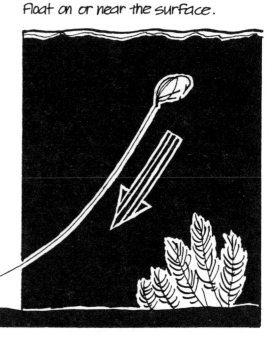

Fishing a leaded shrimp

The combination of lead wire and the shape of the body results in the artificial adopting an inverted attitude, which simulates the natural in a very life-like manner.

This pattern represents the fresh-water shrimp, Gammarus; a resident of well-oxygenated water. They thrive in watercress, suggesting therefore that lakes fed by streams containing this plant would be ideal places to use this very effective little pattern.

A leaded shrimp is ideally suited for margin fishing in clear-water lakes. Let the shrimp sink to the bottom where trout are patrolling.

When a trout approaches, inch the shrimp off the bottom in short jerks.

Midday: June, July and August

Bright, sunny midsummer days are not conducive to good fishing; local anglers, having fished early in the morning, take a siesta until the sun begins to drop westward. For the visiting angler who has limited time, it's Hobson's Choice. However, he should not be disheartened, because although the surface of the lake may look dead, there are areas in the deeper water which hold concentrations of fish.

DAM

Deep water

Shallower water

WIND

Best bank for left—handed angler.

WIND

Best bank for right—handed angler.

If the lake is man-made, the dam end is always a good place to try, especially if the wind is blowing in that direction.

A lure or large nymph on a 9ft (2.75m) leader to a No. 7-8 weight-forward or shooting-head line should make contact with deep-swimming trout.

Trout will be found very close to reservoir dams, but the fly should never be allowed to make contact with the stone or concrete structure, as this may damage the hook point.

Trout will often take a lure as it sinks, therefore positive contact should be maintained from the moment the line hits the water.

Search different depths until the fish are located

If, after a while there is no response, tie on a dropper and fish two lures.

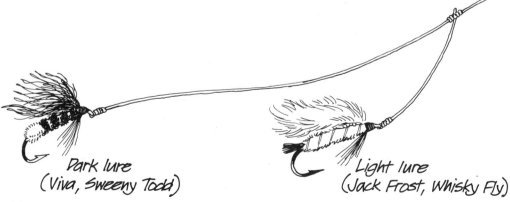

Dark lure
(Viva, Sweeny Todd)

Light lure
(Jack Frost, Whisky Fly)

Variations in retrieve can also mean the difference between success and failure.

(A)

(B)

(C)

(A) LONG STEADY PULLS
(B) SHORT JERKY TWITCHES
(C) SINK AND DRAW

Fish the lure, or lures, to within 1½ rod-lengths from the tip eye of the rod, then lift the rod and pull the lure to the surface—trout will often take at the last minute.

Lures

Ace of Spades

Appetizer

Missionary

Jack Frost

Muddler Minnow

Church Fry

Baby Doll

Polystickle

Sweeny Todd

Whisky Fly

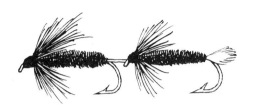

Worm Fly

Black and Orange Marabou

Badger Lure

Black Lure

Dog Nobbler

Jersey Herd

Perch Fry

Undertaker

Matuka

Viva

September and October

Autumn provides two high-lights in the year. Where coarse fish are present, the fry of roach, perch or bream form large shoals, which are continually harassed by marauding trout. Craneflies or daddy longlegs are also in abundance and often blown on to the water, where they are quickly devoured by the trout.

FRY—IMITATING LURES

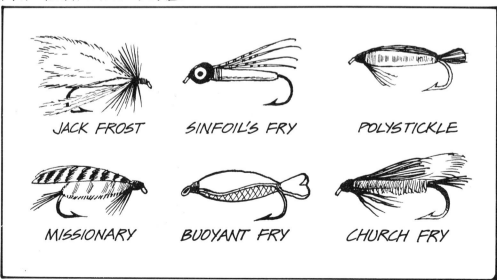

JACK FROST   SINFOIL'S FRY   POLYSTICKLE

MISSIONARY   BUOYANT FRY   CHURCH FRY

The presence of a fry-feeding trout is usually manifested by a disturbance on the surface of the water as the fry attempt to escape the lunges of the predator.

When Fry-feeding trout have been located it is usually just a matter of casting, with a floating or neutral density line, into the area of activity.

VARIOUS WAYS TO PRESENT A FRY LURE

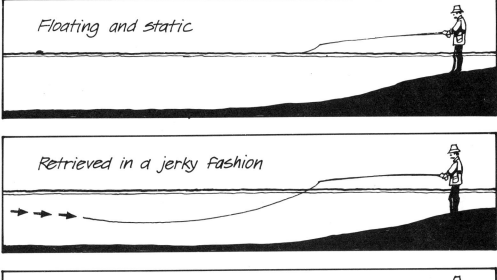

Floating and static

Retrieved in a jerky fashion

Allowed to sink

The boat angler fishing over deep water will stand more chance of contacting the bigger fry-feeding trout.

Run of the mill stock fish up to 2lb (0·90 kg) chasing shoals of fry.

Ultra fast sinking or lead-core line presents lure in big fish area.

Large trout (often browns) wait for easy pickings as wounded and dead fry sink to the bottom.

MISSIONARY (an ideal lure for this method)

Fishing the daddy

Dapping with a natural daddy longlegs (cranefly) has been practised for many years on some Irish and Scottish lochs. Given the right conditions, this form of fishing can be applied to most still water fisheries. There is no need to use the natural insect, either — an artificial 'daddy' works just as well.

WIND

Length of floss line tied to 6lb (2·70kg) main line.

6ft (1·85m) leader B.S. 6lb (2·70 kg)

Fishing an artificial daddy
longlegs from the bank, with
a weight-forward or double-
taper line, can be very
effective in breezy conditions.

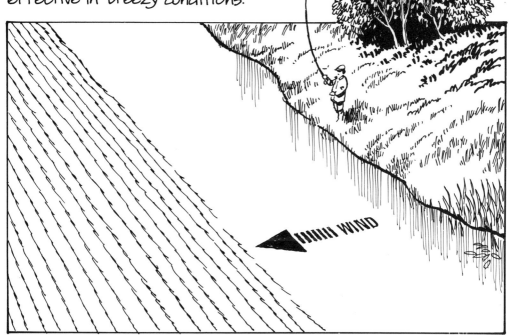

Trout will take a dry daddy
longlegs if it is fished static
in the surface film, but they
seem to respond in a more
positive manner to a fly
which is dragged across the
water surface.

Anatomy of a trout

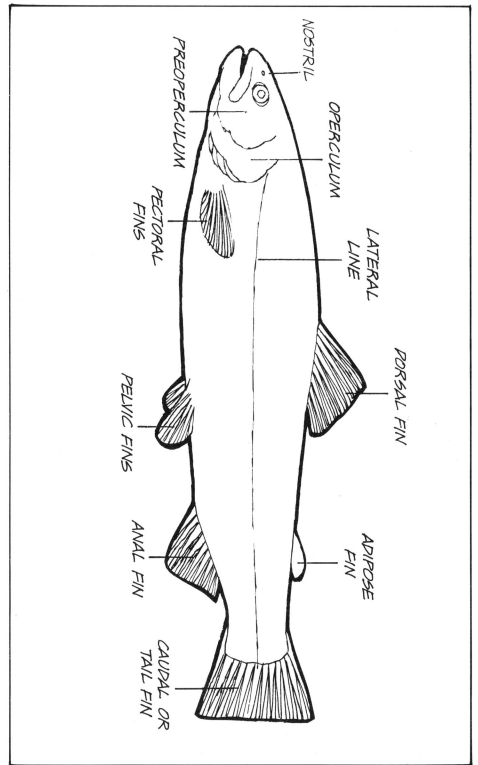

NOSTRIL

PREOPERCULUM

OPERCULUM

PECTORAL FINS

LATERAL LINE

PELVIC FINS

DORSAL FIN

ANAL FIN

ADIPOSE FIN

CAUDAL OR TAIL FIN

Playing and landing a trout

1

As soon as a trout is hooked, hold the rod well up.

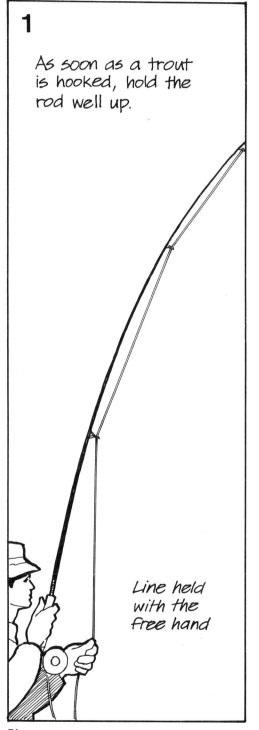

Line held with the free hand

2

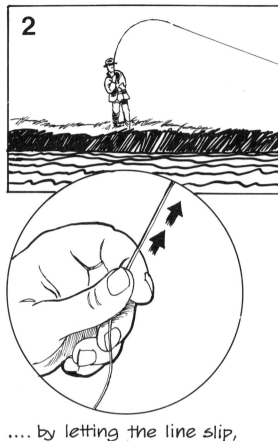

.... by letting the line slip, under pressure, through the index finger and thumb.

4

The fish can now be played from the reel.

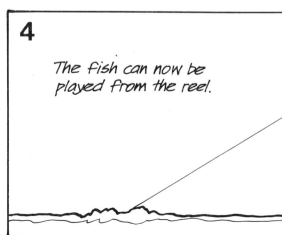

When a trout feels the resistance of the rod and line it will often take off on a powerful run, and should be given its head....

3

At this point, a few backward steps should get rid of any loose coils of line which may have been lying on the bank.

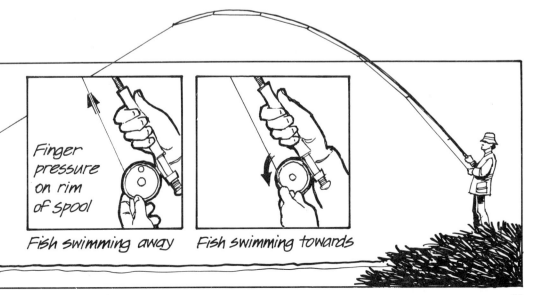

Finger pressure on rim of spool

Fish swimming away

Fish swimming towards

5

Many anglers play a fish directly from the line, and while this is fine up to a point, and very efficient for keeping in touch with a trout which is swimming rapidly towards the angler, there is the problem of having loose coils of line lying on the bank which could become snagged or tangled and result in a lost fish.

The best way to turn a trout away from snags is to apply side strain.

6

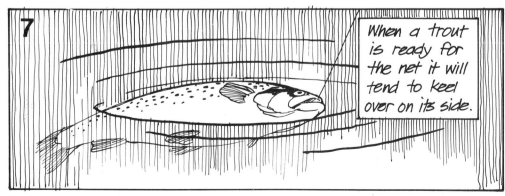

7

When a trout is ready for the net it will tend to keel over on its side.

Draw the fish over the frame of the stationary net. NEVER jab at the fish in an attempt to scoop it out.

Lift the frame clear of the water, draw the net towards the bank and lift, stepping back at the same time. The last three movements should be done in one smooth easy action. Large trout will probably have to be dragged up the bank.

Accessories

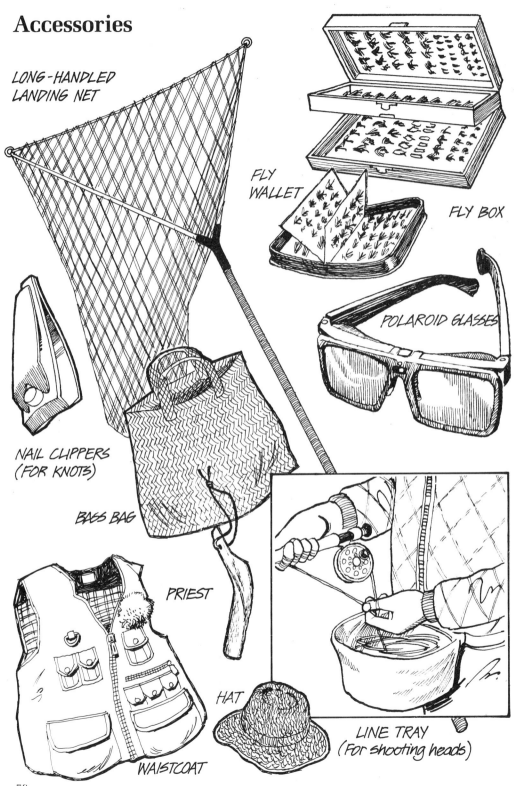

LONG-HANDLED
LANDING NET

FLY
WALLET

FLY BOX

POLAROID GLASSES

NAIL CLIPPERS
(FOR KNOTS)

BASS BAG

PRIEST

HAT

LINE TRAY
(for shooting heads)

WAISTCOAT

Mending a ferrule

Spigot ferrules, especially those on carbon fibre rods, tend to wear loose very quickly.

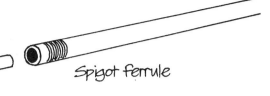

Spigot ferrule

A loose ferrule can be noticed immediately, because the male and female sections are touching one another when the rod is assembled.

To produce a tighter fit, rub the male section with candle wax.

If the ferrule is very badly worn, more drastic measures will have to be taken.

Cut about ¼ in (6 mm) from the female section, then re-whip to provide support.

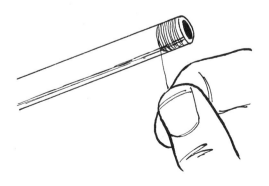

A correctly fitting spigot ferrule should look like this.

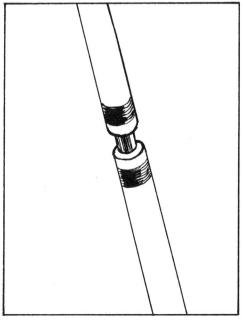